298

Tension Getters

50 Real-Life Problems and Predicaments for Today's Youth

Tension Getters

50 Real-Life Problems and Predicaments
for Today's Youth
by MIKE YACONELLI and DAVID LYNN

A Bible Society Creative Handbook
For churches, teachers, and youth group leaders

BIBLE SOCIETY
Stonehill Green, Westlea, Swindon SN5 7DG, England

This edition issued by special arrangement with Zondervan Publishing House, Grand Rapids, Michigan, U.S.A.
Original title: AMAZING TENSION GETTERS
Copyright © 1988 by Youth Specialties, Inc.

Unless otherwise stated, quotations from the Bible are from the Good News Bible, published by the Bible Societies/Collins, © American Bible Society, New York, 1966, 1971, 1976.

This edition first published 1991 by Bible Society.
Copyright © British and Foreign Bible Society 1991.
Printed in Great Britain by BPCC Wheatons Ltd, Exeter.

British Library Cataloguing in Publication Data

Yaconelli, Mike
  Tension getters.
  1. Christianity: Adolescents: Religious life
  I. Title II. Lynn, David H. *1954*–
  268.433

ISBN 0-564-05765-7

Bible Societies exist to provide resources for Bible distribution and use. Bible Society in England and Wales (BFBS) is a member of the United Bible Societies, an international partnership working in over 180 countries. Their common aim is to reach all people with the Bible, or some part of it, in a language they can understand and at a price they can afford. Parts of the Bible have now been translated into approximately 1,900 languages. Bible Societies aim to help every church at every point where it uses the Bible. You are invited to share in this work by your prayers and gifts. The Bible Society in your country will be very happy to provide details of its activity.

contents

PART ONE: Options
These situations have been formulated to make your
youth group think of all the available options when making
a moral choice.

PART TWO: Opinions
These have been written to reflect the actual feelings of
today's adolescents. Your youth group will be asked to
compare their feelings and opinions with those expressed
in the situations given in the book.

PART THREE: Tensions

The stories in this section require your youth group to think about the way each character in a story behaves.

PART FOUR: Dear diary

These fictional "diary entries" are intimate, no-holds-barred statements of adolescent feelings. Have your youth group read these "confidential" writings and then respond to them.

introduction

Today's youth live in a complex and rapidly changing society. Moral standards that once seemed written in stone are now disintegrating. There seem to be no agreed-upon standards and values. As a result, young people are set adrift in a bewildering sea of moral choices without the aid of a moral compass. They are faced daily with an ever-increasing number of options and alternatives without the assistance of a moral road-map.

In past generations, society agreed upon a widely held set of values. Society rewarded those who went along and penalized those who did not. The cultural norms, more often than not, coincided with biblical norms. Not any longer. Now, young people are being taught that the only norm they can depend on is themselves. "Whatever is right for you" has become the only moral absolute. The result is that moral certainty has been replaced by moral confusion, and the issue in the church has become "How can we help young people make moral choices in a world that presents so many options?" We are faced with the difficult task of preparing our young people to make right decisions in a culture that no longer cares what is right or wrong.

To put the dilemma of the church in practical terms, we must decide how the church is to deal with the issues of the present in the artificial environment of the Sunday School classroom where options seem black and white. As soon as our young people move out of the classroom, they are faced with complex choices that are neither black nor white. They leave the world of simple solutions and enter the real world of not-so-simple solutions.

The problem is one of transfer. The church needs to provide a learning environment where young people can take what they learn in the classroom and apply it to the world outside. If they cannot transfer what they learn, then it won't be long until they become frustrated and decide to abandon their faith because it does not seem relevant to life. That is why we have written *Tension Getters.*

This is a book of strategies designed specifically to help your young people transfer what they have learned in the classroom to daily life. Each strategy has been chosen for its close resemblance to real-life situations and issues. We hope that when your young people encounter similar situations in the real world, they can transfer the knowledge and skills acquired while using these strategies. Helping young people be prepared for decisions in the real world is the function of *Tension Getters*. Here's how it works:

Tension Getters Create Tension

Each strategy in this book has been included because of its potential to create a dilemma or situation with conflicting issues that require young people to think through all possible alternatives and consequences before arriving at a moral decision. Tension is created when there is an overlap of values that make a simple black-and-white response impossible. Most decisions in the real world require sifting through layers of values before a choice is made. For example, let's suppose a young person is asked to help a friend cheat on a test. The student is torn between friendship with the friend, friendship with the other students, the personal value of honesty, and so on. A diagram would look like this:

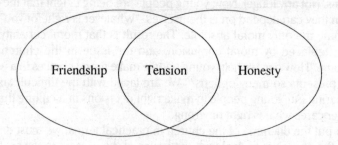

Where these values overlap is the area of tension. A decision must be made in the midst of the reality that all of these values are present at the same time. The issue is to decide which value has priority in the presence of all other values, rather than deciding which one is right or which one is wrong. Recreating this tension helps young people think through their value system and become conscious of its implications in real-life situations.

Tension Getters Require an Atmosphere of Growth

One of the biggest obstacles to overcome with young people in the church is their preconceived idea that church is where you learn all the right answers. Because we believe the Christian faith is the ultimate answer to the problems of life, young people misunderstand this to mean that it provides a specific answer to each particular problem in life. The Christian faith does provide a foundation upon which young people can build in their dealings with the particulars of life, but they must learn how to discover those particulars themselves. For that reason, *Tension Getters* does not provide answers; it creates questions – the kind of healthy questions that lead to growth.

Growth will only occur if there is an atmosphere of neutral openness. That does not mean the leader or the church is neutral on important issues; it simply means that the leader allows freedom for all points of view to be expressed without judgement. It's important to make the young person feel that what matters more than the right answer is *their* answer. Here's how to create this kind of atmosphere:

1. Open-ended discussion

It's important not to push or force the group's discussion to a conclusion. Certainly the group should stay on the subject, but you don't need to resolve all the loose ends in 45 minutes. Discussion is squelched when young people feel pressure to end on time and to resolve all issues. The emphasis ought to be on having as many options as possible so that, when the decision is made, it is made with all of the alternatives in mind.

2. Freedom to say what one thinks

Young people are often penalized if they say what they really think, especially if what they say is opposed to what the church or the leader thinks. Because this makes them reluctant to express their real feelings, it's important for you to affirm legitimate expressions of opinion no matter what the content. Remember that allowing young people to say what they believe does not mean that you agree or approve of their ideas. It simply means that you approve of their right to express their ideas and submit them for discussion.

The best response to any comment is to show interest and ask for more. Probe in a non-threatening manner; ask why they believe the way they do. Push them to follow their ideas to their logical consequence; then let those ideas sink or swim on their own merits. If you feel that it's necessary to respond to their ideas, you can always do so later, when giving your concluding remarks.

3. Recreating the realities of life

Three ingredients have to be present in a discussion if you are to simulate a real-life situation:

Situations involving real people

It's much easier for young people to defend "Tom" than to defend their own personal belief system. They don't feel threatened when discussing other people's beliefs – but, in reality, when they talk about the Tom in the story, they are telling you what they believe. Through a story about someone else, they are actually expressing their own value system.

Complex characters

The characters in *Tension Getters* have good qualities and bad qualities. There is enough of a mix of good and bad, just like in real life, to make a simplistic response impossible. It's easy to decide who is right when someone is all good like the Lone Ranger, but in real life all people are a mixture of good and bad – like the ordinary people in the strategies in this book.

Mixture of consequences

Tension Getters are constructed in such a way that whatever decisions are made have both good and bad consequencies; they help one person while hurting another. That, too, is like life – even the best decisions usually hurt someone.

how to use tension getters

Tension Getters is participant-centred rather than leader-centred. If you want to use these strategies successfully, all members of the group need to be encouraged to participate. You must foster a climate that is conducive to discussion by communicating that each person's opinion is worthwhile and that each person has a responsibility within the group to contribute to the solutions. For these strategies to have any meaning, there must be a variety of opinions and viewpoints.

Starting the Discussion

Pass out to each person a copy of the strategy to be discussed, along with a pencil and extra paper for note-taking. Tell the group that the strategy given is the total story – they can't add, subtract, or ask "what if?" questions. They're to deal with the story as it is.

When everyone has read the story, divide the group (if it's large enough) into small sections of five to seven. Have each group assign a facilitator* to keep the discussion moving and a recorder to keep a record of the decision made so they can be reported to the larger group. Have the facilitator start the discussion by merely asking the questions that accompany the *Tension Getters*. The group then discusses the questions and attempts to arrive at one or more conclusions. If a group appears to be stymied, you may want to get them back on the track by throwing out some new ideas, playing the devil's advocate, or attempting to summarize what has already been discussed.

Ending the Discussion

When all the options have been explored, it's time to make some decisions. If you have more than one group, then each group should

---

*The facilitator should be one of the young people. If, however, you have several adult youth leaders, you may wish to have each one assigned to a different group. Make sure each leader becomes an equal member of the group. They shouldn't dominate, and if the group looks to the leader for "the answer", have the leader direct the question back to the group.

arrive at a consensus. If any group can't find a consensus, the members should compile minority reports. Each group should choose someone – perhaps their recorder – to present their report to the larger group.

Allow all views to be shared; allow the larger group to discuss these views after they've been expressed. Now's the time for you to exercise your options about how complicated you want the discussion to become, and how much closure you want to bring to it. You may want to leave the topic hanging until the following week and encourage the young people to talk to their parents or others. This gives the young people time to digest all the implications of the issues raised during the discussion. Or you may want to complicate the discussion by adding new information to the story, such as: "What if Tom were a Christian?" or "What if Linda had only six months to live?" Sometimes, those complications are needed in order to meet the specific needs of your group. There may be times when you want to summarize the discussion and use it as a springboard for a teaching opportunity. Finally, you can allow the questions raised during the discussion to go unanswered, allowing the youth group to wrestle with the issues on their own.

Using Scripture

Each of the strategies in this book is followed by Bible references. These references were selected for their relevance to the particular strategy and for their potential to generate healthy discussion and to stimulate dialogue. They are not to be considered exhaustive. You'll probably think of other applicable passages; feel free to add whatever Scriptures you believe are equally relevant. None of the Scriptures listed are intended to provide "the answer" to the ethical dilemma you're discussing. Instead, they're there to shed light on the situation and to give practical guidance by focusing on the question, "What does God say about this?". It's important not to abuse the Bible by using any of these passages out of context, and it's also important not to deal with the difficult decisions in life without the input of Scripture. The passages listed are just the tip of the iceberg, inviting you to "search the Scriptures" and dig deeper.

Here are some suggestions to help you use the Scripture references effectively:

1. Read the Scriptures out loud together. It's important for the group to focus on the Scriptures together so all the members can deal with the biblical implications for the strategy being discussed.

2. Examine each Scripture separately, checking the context to see what effect it has on the meaning. Encourage the group to come to an agreement on the meaning of the passage, and then apply that

meaning to the strategy you're discussing. Does it have any relevance? How does it affect your decision?

3. Examine all the Scriptures you are using together; encourage the group to summarize the relationship of the passages. For example, after reading a number of passages relating to adultery, the group's summary statement might be, "Although God is against adultery, he also seems to treat the adulterer with love". Apply your summary statement to the strategy you are discussing. How does it affect your decision?

Be prepared for the fact that some Scriptures will actually make the decision-making process more difficult. There are many Scriptures that seem to present opposing viewpoints on the same issue. Whether that's true or not, we have not used Scripture as a gimmick. We have tried to honestly present relevant Scriptures (whether they speak clearly or vaguely) with the knowledge that "all Scripture is profitable", and that God's Word "will not return to him void".

when to use
tension getters

Tension Getters is not a curriculum. It isn't designed to be used every week – in fact, it's most effective when it's used to supplement the larger unit of curriculum you're using. It isn't a book full of gimmicks or quickie programmes that will keep your young people busy for an hour. This book is full of individual strategies that can stand alone or be used with others, and can meet a variety of needs if used properly. Here are some suggestions.

Discussion Starters

A primary function of *Tension Getters* is to create lively discussion. Each strategy is a story, and almost all of them relate to situations similar to those your young people encounter every day. As a result, you can expect high interest. In other words, rather than beginning your youth meeting with "What do you think about cheating?", you can start with a story about Tom, the school athletics captain, who asks a friend to help with a test. Everyone in your youth group will have an opinion.

Spiritual Thermometer

As you observe the discussion generated by *Tension Getters*, you can discover, in a non-threatening atmosphere, what your young people believe. By observing them during the entire process of decision making, you can know not only what the kids in your youth group believe but how they got there. This is invaluable for the youth leader who wants to know his or her students and understand what their needs are. If the content of your programme is based on the needs of your youth, *Tension Getters* should become an integral part of your programme.

These strategies are also effective in helping your young people discover what they really believe. One such strategy was used at a young-adult conference a few years ago. Before the strategy was used, everyone was asked if they believed in situational ethics. Not one person admitted that he or she did. After discussing a strategy which involved the issues of situational ethics, over fifty per cent of the conference realized that they did believe in situational ethics, at least in this instance. This knowledge was not only invaluable for those who participated, but also for the leaders who could then focus on that particular issue.

Creative Alternatives

Although *Tension Getters* is full of strategies that are great discussion starters, there are many other possibilities. You can use these strategies to introduce a role play, to stimulate some creative writing, or to set the scene for a skit or dramatic situation. The possibilities are endless once young people are motivated.

You will find one other advantage to these strategies: They create tangent issues. Because these strategies deal with many different values at the same time, you will often find your young people talking about something other than the main topic. In the process of the discussion, they have focused on a tangent issue. Sometimes, you'll want to get them back to the main topic, but often you'll want to pursue the tangent issue because it expresses a need you weren't aware of.

caution

Remember that you are the final authority when it comes to programming for your youth group. You are the one who must decide whether your group needs more tension at this time, whether they are mature enough to hear all the alternatives, and whether they are spiritually able to deal with conflict. Here are some guidelines to keep in mind:

1. Know your young people

Some young people are not ready to handle certain problems. You might have planned to discuss the issue of death, but because one of your young people has a parent who is dying, it may not be the time to discuss that subject. It might also be the perfect time – but to make that decision you have to know your young people well.

2. Don't throw them in at the deep end

There are many issues of our faith that are difficult for even adults to handle. Be careful not to shoot down all of their arguments just to create conflict. As young people mature, they not only learn more, but they learn to handle more ambiguity. Make sure your young people are getting a lot of positive content along with content that creates tension.

3. Don't try to shock young people for effect

If you play the devil's advocate, make sure your arguments are sensible. In other words, don't become so artificial in your role as spoiler that the group doesn't take your point of view seriously. Sometimes leaders try to shock kids with extreme arguments or positions that, more often than not, have a reverse effect. The young people treat the discussion more like a skit and the discussion degenerates into a meaningless exchange.

4. Give people time

Don't feel that every issue must be resolved in 60 minutes. Let the young people go home thinking. Let issues stay unresolved for a while. It takes time to think through issues, and when young people are carrying unresolved issues, they usually end up talking with someone about them, like their parents or friends. That dialogue can be very productive.

Don't be afraid of controversy or failure

When you create tension, deal with controversial issues, send people home with issues unresolved, or disturb beliefs that people are comfortable with, you are going to generate criticism from young people as well as from parents. Sometimes the criticism will be justified, because sometimes you will make mistakes. Sometimes you may even lose a young person, but those are the risks of good education. Admit your mistakes, learn from your failures, but don't back off simply because you have pushed people into new areas of growth and maturity.

We think you will find *Tension Getters* an invaluable resource. Enjoy this book. Use it wisely, selectively, and prayerfully. We hope you will find it to be a significant contribution to your youth group's spiritual growth and development.

part one:
options

These situations have been formulated to cause your youth group to think of all the available options when making a moral choice. Your group will be asked to choose one particular option over the others and explain why that option was chosen.

1. Violent dilemma

Susan is sixteen and is totally confused. She has known for a long time that her father physically abuses her mother, but she has felt helpless to do anything. Susan's mother absolutely refuses to talk about it and doesn't allow Susan to tell anyone. "I love your father, and if you tell someone, it might mean your father would go to prison." Well, Susan doesn't want her father to go to prison, nor does she want to cause her mother any more pain.

But last night was too much. Her father came home in a very ugly mood; he not only beat her mother severely, but he also tried to hurt Susan. She ran out of the house and came to you. She wants to know what to do.

- What are Susan's options?
- What would you advise her to do? Why?

Suggested scripture to read

Matthew 18.21–35   *The parable of the unforgiving servant*
1 Peter 3.1–7; 7–17 *Wives and husbands; Suffering for doing right*
Proverbs 11.17   *"If you are cruel you only hurt yourself"*

For further study or reflection

Luke 17.3a–4   *"If your brother sins . . ."*
2 Corinthians 2.5–10   *"Forgiveness for the offender"*
Romans 12.14–21   *"Ask God to bless those who persecute you . . ."*

2. Christmas in Tenerife

Paula's parents have been divorced for five years now. Her father has remarried and lives out of the area. Paula lives with her mother and sees her father once or twice a year. Her mother has never remarried. Now that Paula is in secondary school, she notices that her mother is increasingly uncomfortable with Paula's trips to see her father. Her mother has never made an issue out of the trips – until now.

To make things worse, Paula has been invited to go to Tenerife with her father and stepmother during the Christmas school break. Paula's mother doesn't want her to go. She says she will have to spend Christmas all alone – and after all the horrible things her father has done, he is the one who should be alone. All Paula knows is that she loves her mother and wouldn't want to hurt either of them. She comes to you for advice.

- What are Paula's options?
- What would you advise her to do? Why?

Suggested scripture to read

Ruth 1   *Naomi and Ruth return to Bethlehem*
Malachi 2.13–16   *Divorce*
Proverbs 11.17   *"If you are cruel you only hurt yourself"*
Ephesians 6.21–33   *Wives and husbands*
1 Corinthians 7.12–16   *Questions about marriage*

3. Big sister/big problem

Belinda's sister is ruining her life. Belinda is fifteen and her sister, Teresa, is twenty-one. Teresa is severely mentally handicapped. Because Belinda's parents both work, she ends up having to take care of Teresa a lot. Belinda knows she shouldn't feel resentment, but she does. She wishes her parents would put Teresa in a special home, but they won't even consider it. The way Teresa acts embarrasses Belinda and her friends. Belinda can tell that her friends don't like to come over anymore. In fact, she sometimes feels as if her friends wonder about her.

Belinda feels more than resentment – she is beginning to hate her sister. She knows she needs to do something. She comes to you for help.

- What are Belinda's options?
- What would you advise her to do? Why?

Suggested scripture to read

Genesis 45.1–5   *Joseph tells his brothers who he is*
Matthew 5.43–48   *Love for enemies*
2 Corinthians 12.7–10   *"My power is strongest when you are weak"*

For further study or reflection

John 15.12   *"Love one another just as I love you"*
Romans 12.3–1   *"Love must be completely sincere"*
John 21.15–24   *"Take care of my sheep"*

4. Family ties

Richard's family has seen noticeable changes in his life since he became a Christian. He has stopped going round with the trouble makers at school. His work has improved. Overall, he seems to be a reformed character except for one problem.

Richard's family is very close. They have always spent a lot of time together. But now that Richard is involved in the church, it seems he's out all the time at some church activity – Sunday morning, Sunday night, Wednesday night, and almost every weekend. When Richard is home the family feels uncomfortable. Mum and Dad watch their language and everyone is uneasy, waiting for Richard to say something religious.

Richard's parents have told him that they don't mind his new faith, as long as he keeps it to himself. But they do mind him being out so much. They feel he's become a stranger in the house, and that he's losing touch with his brothers and sisters. So, last night, they told him that he has to cut back on church activities and stay at home during the week. He can attend church once on Sunday, and that's all.

Richard was devastated. He not only wants to go to the youth group, he needs them. He knows that if he stops going, he'll be right back where he was a few months ago. He comes to you for help.

- What are Richard's options?
- What would you advise him to do? Why?

Suggested scripture to read

Matthew 5.1–6   *The Sermon on the Mount*
Luke 14.25–27   *The cost of being a disciple*
Mark 6.1–6   *Jesus is rejected at Nazareth*
Matthew 10.34–39   *Not peace, but a sword*

5. Dad gambles

Some dads fish, some dads hunt, but Gary's dad gambles. For as long as Gary can remember, Mr Garner has put money on horses and done the pools. Most of the time his dad would lose – only up to a certain amount and then he would quit. But every once in a while he would win, and those were wonderful times. Gary's dad would take the whole family out to dinner, and there would be a big family celebration with surprise gifts for everyone.

Gary's family is active in a local church. A week ago, he was invited to a friend's church to hear a guest speaker. The topic of his sermon was "Why God Dislikes Gambling". Gary was really surprised. It had never occurred to him that gambling might be wrong. Gary knew there were people who were addicted to gambling, and he understood how it could be wrong for some people. But this speaker was saying that no Christian should gamble. Ever. For any reason. Now Gary is confused. He comes to you for advice.

■ What are Gary's options?
■ What would you advise him to do? Why?

Suggested scripture to read

Matthew 6.24–34   *God and possessions*
Romans 14.1–12   *Do not judge your brother*
1 John 2.15–17   *The new command*

Junior   26/8/05
Senior.

6. Older man/younger woman

Melissa is in the 4th year at Warnebrook Comprehensive. She's fifteen, but looks much older. Her mother has made it clear that Melissa can't go out with 6th form boys, and that has never been a problem – until now. Pete is gorgeous. He's also a Christian, active in the youth fellowship and a lot of fun.

Melissa isn't the type to deceive her parents. She and her mum have a good relationship, and she feels sure her mum will understand. So Melissa asks her if she can go out with Pete. The answer is no.

Melissa can't believe it. Her mum won't listen to reason. Melissa wants to do what her mum says, and she doesn't want to damage their relationship, but she doesn't want to lose Pete. She comes to you for help.

- What are Melissa's options?
- What would you advise her to do? Why?

Suggested scripture to read

Ecclesiastes 11.9–10   *Advice to young people*
Ephesians 6.1–4   *Children and parents*
Colossians 3.18–4.1   *"It is your Christian duty to obey your parents always"*

7. Who to tell?

Fifteen months ago Denise had an abortion. It was an emotionally horrifying experience that took Denise almost a year of counselling to get over. Denise now feels that abortion is wrong and believes that God has forgiven her. She has been trying to get on with her life.

For the past few months, Denise has been getting pretty serious with a new boyfriend, Graham. He's great – one of those rare people nowadays who have standards. They've had some wonderful talks, and Graham has made it clear what he thinks about abortion. He hates the thought of it.

Denise is miserable because the more serious she gets with Graham, the more she feels the need to tell him what she's done. He might find out anyway – her old boyfriend knows, and her best girlfriend knows. They've been sworn to secrecy, but you never know. And if Graham found out from someone else, well, that could be a disaster. Denise comes to you for advice.

- What are Denise's options?
- What would you advise her to do? Why?

Suggested scripture to read

Matthew 10.26–31   *Who to fear*
1 John 3.19–24   *Courage before God*
1 John 4.16b–18   *"There is no fear in love"*

8. Good friend to a bad friend

Samantha and Christine have been good friends for a long time. But Samantha has changed over the last year, and not for the better. She has stopped going to church, started working at a burger restaurant most evenings, bought a motorbike, taken up smoking, and is known to drink quite a bit at parties. She's still the bubbly, fun person she always was. She says that she's outgrown the church and religion, but nothing else has changed. That isn't quite true – everyone else has seen the change in Samantha, including her parents and Christine's parents, and no one likes it.

Samantha's parents are concerned and have asked Christine to stick with Samantha and try to help her. That was fine with Christine – until last week, when her own parents sat her down and said they didn't want her hanging around Samantha anymore. They thought Samantha was a bad influence on her. Christine had to admit to herself that Samantha had influenced her negatively lately, but not enough to be a problem. Christine doesn't know what to do. She wants to be Samantha's friend, but her parents say absolutely not. Christine comes to you for advice.

■ What are Christine's options?
■ What would you advise her to do? Why?

Suggested scripture to read

Luke 6.37–42   *Judging others*
Philippians 2.1–11   *"Look out for one another's interests"*
1 Corinthians 5.9–13   *"It is none of my business to judge outsiders"*
Philemon 4–22   *"At one time he was of no use to you but now he is useful both to you and me"*

9. The boy who wouldn't give up

Jill and Gordon had been going out together for three years. From the beginning, Jill knew the relationship had problems, but she kept thinking that either they'd break up or things would get better. But things didn't get better, nor did they break up. Gordon became more and more possessive and demanding. Finally, when Jill left school, she told Gordon it was over. Gordon was devastated – he had thought they were getting married. He cried, pleaded, and became very angry, but Jill stuck to her decision.

Then Gordon began phoning her at home every night and at work every morning. Jill refused to talk to him. He would follow her home from work and try to talk to her. One night at 2 a.m., Jill heard a knocking at her window. It was Gordon. Jill called her father and he firmly convinced Gordon that coming around at 2 a.m. was not a good idea. Still Gordon persisted.

Then Jill got the letter. Gordon said that he loved her very much. He said he couldn't understand how she could have encouraged their physical relationship and now act like that didn't matter. He closed by telling Jill that if she didn't come back to him, he didn't know what he would do. He might even kill himself. It was up to her. This letter hurt Jill. She certainly didn't want to be responsible for Gordon committing suicide. She comes to you for advice.

- What are Jill's options?
- What would you advise her to do?

Suggested scripture to read

1 Corinthians 13.4–13   *Love*
1 John 4.16b–18   *God is love*
Judges 1.4–22   *Samson and Delilah*

For further study or reflection

Proverbs 24.26   *"An honest answer is a sign of true friendship"*

10. Little sister

It's hard when you're the first child. Especially if you're a girl. Your parents try to keep you from growing up as long as they can. Laura can still remember every row she had with her parents about growing up. A row when she wanted to wear short skirts, a row when she wanted to wear make-up, a row over getting her ears pierced, then a row over the size of her earrings. But now her little sister, Lesley, is growing up and it seems she's allowed to do anything she wants. She's just twelve, and already she's wearing lip gloss, big earrings, and high heels. She looks like a miniature twenty-year-old. Laura has brought this up with her parents several times, but they deny that Lesley is getting away with anything. Laura is resentful and feels cheated. Now her parents are telling her she can't drive alone until she's eighteen. Laura blows up at her parents and walks out. She comes to your house. She wants to know what to do.

- What are Laura's options?
- What would you advise her to do? Why?

Suggested scripture to read

Luke 15.11–32   *The lost son*
Mark 9.33–37   *Who is the greatest?*
Luke 14.7–14   *"When you are invited, go and sit in the lowest place"*

For further study or reflection

1 Peter 5.1–7   *"God resists the proud but shows favour to the humble"*
James 3.13–18   *"Where there is jealousy . . . there is disorder"*

11. Hunchback

Sarah kept staring at the mirror. She had known for the last few months that something was wrong, but she hadn't been able to work out what. Now she knew. There was something very wrong with her back. Her shoulders weren't even, and her back seemed to have a slight curve to it. Sarah wanted to believe that it was just an illusion, that she was being a hypochondriac – but she couldn't deny it anymore.

Sarah told her parents. After the doctor's examination, he explained that about 10 percent of all teenagers have some form of scoliosis, or curvature of the spine. He explained that if Sarah would wear a brace for three years, the scoliosis could be eliminated – or at least slowed to the point where no one would notice. But Sarah would have to wear the brace conscientiously. Then the doctor showed her the brace. It was horrible. Sarah began to cry. No more swimming, bikinis, tennis. She would look like a freak for three years. Sarah made up her mind right then that she would not wear that brace. God could make it so that she didn't have to wear the brace – he could heal her. Certainly he wouldn't want her to look like a freak during her teenage years, would he? She comes to you for advice.

- What are Sarah's options?
- What would you advise her to do? Why?

Suggested scripture to read

2 Corinthians 12.1–10   *"My grace is all you need . . ."*
Acts 3.1–10   *A lame man is healed*
Isaiah 52.13–15   *The suffering servant*
John 14.12–13   *"If you ask for anything in my name, I will do it"*
1 Corinthians 6.12–20   *"Your body is the temple of the Holy Spirit"*

For further study or reflection

Psalm 77   *Comfort in time of distress*

12. The loner

Jim wasn't stupid. He knew what everyone thought of him. The mirror doesn't lie – Jim wasn't very good looking. Ha! That was a laugh; he was just plain odd-looking. Everyone made fun of him. He wished he could say, "Well, I may be ugly, but at least I come top in every class", or "Go ahead, I've got loadsa money, so why should I care if I don't have any friends?". But Jim's parents didn't have much money and his school work was average. Jim was simply the kind of person no one wanted to be with. All Jim wanted was a friend. That wasn't too much to ask, was it? Jim was very lonely – and, since you're the only one in the class who even says "hello", he's come to you for advice.

- What are Jim's options?
- What would you advise him to do? Why?

Suggested scripture to read

Luke 19.1–10   *Jesus and Zacchaeus*
Psalm 139   *God's complete knowledge and care*
Isaiah 43.1–7   *"I have called you by your name . . . you are mine"*

—— part two: ——
opinions

These opinions have been written to reflect the actual feelings of many of today's adolescents. Your youth group will be asked to compare their feelings and opinions with those expressed in the situations given in the book.

13. This can't be happening

I can't believe it. My parents are getting a divorce. My mum says it's because Dad's working all the time and doesn't care about her. But what about me? It seems as though neither of them cares about me. Why do they have to do this now? It's really messing up my exams, in fact my whole life. They could have waited until I was out of the house and at college. Of course, I knew they weren't happy, but so what? At least I was happy. Now we're all unhappy. Besides, they can move or get another job, but what can I do? Change schools in my 'A' level year? Get a job? Give us a break. I am really angry at my parents for being so selfish that they can't even think of their own child and what this is doing to him.

Rick, 18

- How would you feel if you were in Rick's position?
- Why do you think you would feel that way?

Suggested scripture to read

Job 7.1–11   *"I am angry and bitter. I have to speak"*
1 Corinthians 13.1–7   *Love*
James 3.13–18   *The wisdom from above*
Ephesians 4.25–32   *"Get rid of all bitterness, passion and anger"*
1 Corinthians 7.10–16   *Questions about marriage*

14. Cover-up

Listen; I'm not stupid. I like good-looking girls as much as anyone else. I mean, I'm going out with Jenny, who's got to be the best-looking girl in our school. But I'm not going out with her just because of her body; I like her. But I know what the lads think, so I care about what she wears in public. For instance, I don't like her wearing bikinis or really short skirts either. My friends think I'm stupid and old-fashioned. They love staring at girls in skimpy clothing, but they would never want to go with a girl like that.

Eddie, 17

How do you feel about Eddie's statement?

Strongly agree	Agree	Neutral	Disagree	Strongly disagree

- If you agree, what would you add to the statement above?
- If you disagree, why?

Suggested scripture to read

Genesis 3.1–12 *The disobedience of man*
1 Peter 3.1–4 *Wives and husbands*
Matthew 5.27–30 *Teaching about adultery*
Matthew 7.1–5 *Judging others*

15. Change of mind

Up till about 3 years ago, I thought people who took drugs were stupid. I still do if you're talking about junkies. But now I think drugs are just like anything else – if you abuse them they're bad; if you don't abuse them, they can be OK. I smoke a joint now and then, but not during school, or even every time there's a party. Just once in a while. It's not as bad as everyone says. My parents would kill me if they knew I had ever smoked before. But, they're hypocrites; they drink and that's no different.

Steve, 17

How do you feel about Steve's statement?

Strongly   Agree   Neutral   Disagree   Strongly
agree   disagree

■ If you agree, what would you add to the statement above?
■ If you disagree, why?

Suggested scripture to read

1 Corinthians 6.12–20   *"Your body is the temple of the Holy Spirit"*
Romans 14.1–10   *Do not judge your brother*

16. Be true to your friends

Look. Everyone lies. It's just part of being a teenager. If by lying you can keep your parents happy and keep your school and your life under control, then why not? I don't mean that it's OK to lie all the time. And I don't think you should lie to your friends, because once you do that and your friends find out – well, you won't have any friends. Here's the way I see it. When you're at school, if it's not your parents getting at you it's the teachers. You have to lie to keep them off your back. The only protection you and I have against all that pressure is to lie once in a while.

Brenda, 17

How do you feel about Brenda's statement?

| Strongly agree | Agree | Neutral | Disagree | Strongly disagree |

■ If you agree, what would you add to the statement above?
■ If you disagree, why?

Suggested scripture to read

Zechariah 8.14–17   *"Speak the truth to one another"*
Ephesians 4.22–25   *The new life in Christ*
Jeremiah 9.2–6   *"Dishonesty instead of truth rules the land"*
Colossians 3.8–11   *The old life and the new*
Matthew 15.10–20   *"The things that come from the heart"*

17. Never admit more than they know

This is the way I look at it. When your mum or dad, a teacher, or another adult confronts you or starts questioning you about something they think you've done, deny it all at first. Then, if they confront you with some obvious fact, admit to that, but nothing else. Deny everything else. For example, if my parents came in and accused me of getting home late the night before, the discussion would go something like this:

Parents: What time did you get in last night, David? You were supposed to be home at half-eleven.

David: I was home at half-eleven, or maybe ten minutes later. I didn't look at my watch.

Parents: It must have been more than ten minutes, David, because I woke up at midnight and checked and you still weren't home.

David Well, it might have been that late, but I know I left the party long before half-eleven so I'd be home on time.

Parents: Was anyone drinking at the party?

David: I don't know.

Parents: Mrs Johnson said she sent some lads home because they were drinking out on the front lawn.

David: Maybe – I don't know. I was inside the house the whole time.

It works every time. Only admit what they know and deny everything else.

David, 16

How do you feel about David's statement?

Strongly agree	Agree	Neutral	Disagree	Strongly disagree

- If you agree, what would you add to the statement above?
- If you disagree, why?

Suggested scripture to read

Jeremiah 9.2–6   *"Dishonesty instead of truth rules the land"*
Colossians 3.8–1   *The old life and the new*
Matthew 15.10–20   *"The things that come out of the mouth come from the heart"*
Ephesians 4.22–25   *The new life in Christ*
Zechariah 8.14–17   *"Speak the truth to one another"*

18. Laid back

I think Christianity is great. Seriously, I think it's fine – as long as you don't get too obsessed with it. I like the youth fellowship; it's a lot of fun. We have a fantastic youth leader and superb programme, and that's all great. But when they start saying we ought to tell our friends about God all the time, and go to church every week, and go to the mission field – I mean really, who's got time for that stuff? You can do that when you're older. Besides, as long as youth fellowship or church keeps you off the streets and gives you a good time, what else do you need? If someone wants to be a minister some day, great; but I don't think I should feel guilty just because I don't want to. When you're at school, you have a lot to do – and church ought to be a part of what you do; but that's it, only a part. Life is a lot more than going to church.

Roger, 16

How do you feel about Roger's statement?

Strongly agree	Agree	Neutral	Disagree	Strongly disagree

■ If you agree, what would you add to the statement?
■ If you disagree, why?

Suggested scripture to read

Luke 18.18–30   *The rich man*
Matthew 25.31–46   *The final judgement*
Romans 12.1–2   *"Let God transform you inwardly"*

19. What's important?

What's it all about? I'll tell you. Making money. It always makes people angry when I say that, but they only get angry because it's true. Making a living, that's it. That's the bottom line. You've got to have money to buy a car, have nice clothes, get a flat or a house, and do fun things. That's what life is about. Who runs the country? Who runs the churches? Who runs everything? The people with the money, that's who. Anyone who tells you anything else is a liar.

Mick, 16

How do you feel about Mick's statement?

| Strongly agree | Agree | Neutral | Disagree | Strongly disagree |

- If you agree, what would you add to the statement above?
- If you disagree, why?

Suggested scripture to read

Matthew 6.24–34   *God and possessions*
Luke 12.13–21   *The parable of the rich fool*
Luke 16.19–31   *The rich man and Lazarus*

20. The end of the world

To listen to adults talk, you would think all the teenagers in the world were sitting around afraid that the world is about to end. What a joke. None of my friends sit around worrying about a nuclear holocaust or the Greenhouse effect. They do worry they won't get their slice of the cake but that's about it. We're not particularly anti-nuclear or anti-aerosols. All we care about is that we get to grow up and have a good time; whatever keeps us from doing that, we're against.

Serena, 15

How do you feel about Serena's statement?

Strongly   Agree   Neutral   Disagree   Strongly
agree   disagree

- If you agree, what would you add to the statement above?
- If you disagree, why?

Suggested scripture to read

Luke 6.20–26   *Happiness and sorrow*
Isaiah 24.1–16   *The Lord will punish the earth*
Revelation 21.1–4   *The new heaven and the new earth*

21. Negative outlook

Every time I do something wrong, my parents remind me of all the things I've done wrong in the last two years. They never forget and seldom forgive. They always focus on the negative. I can do everything I am supposed to for three weeks in a row and they never say a word, but if I make one mistake I never stop hearing about it. I don't think they've ever said a positive thing to me. It doesn't matter what I do – they're never satisfied.

Malcolm, 14

- How would you feel if you were in Malcolm's position?
- Why do you think you would feel that way?

Suggested scripture to read

Romans 12   *Life in God's service*
Matthew 5.43–48   *Love for enemies*
Matthew 6.19–21   *Riches in heaven*
Colossians 3.21   *"Parents, do not irritate your children"*

22. It's my body

It's my body. I don't understand why my parents think they can tell me what to do with my body. When it comes to my hairstyle, or wearing an earring, or any other part of my personal appearance, I think that should be my choice, not my parents'. I'm old enough now to know what's good for me and what isn't. Besides, I don't usually get into arguments with my parents about what's good for me; it's usually just a matter of taste. And my taste is just as "right" as theirs.

Tim, 15

How do you feel about Tim's statement?

Strongly agree	Agree	Neutral	Disagree	Strongly disagree

■ If you agree, what would you add to the statement above?
■ If you disagree, why?

Suggested scripture to read

1 Samuel 15.1–13   *"Man looks at the outward appearance but I look at the heart"*
Proverbs 19.20   *"If you listen to advice . . ."*
Proverbs 12.15   *"Stupid people always think they are right"*

23. I don't want to die

I don't care what they say in church about heaven, I don't want to die. It may be great up there, but I like it here just fine. I don't want to go to heaven yet. I don't want to sit around with a load of angels. I want to live and have fun here and now. If that means I'm not a Christian, then I guess I'm not a Christian. Because I don't think anyone should want to die rather than live.

Shirley, 16

How do you feel about Shirley's statement?

Strongly   Agree   Neutral   Disagree   Strongly
agree   disagree

■ If you agree, what would you add to the statement above?
■ If you disagree, why?

Suggested scripture to read

Ecclesiastes 3.1–13   *A time for everything*
John 14.1–4   *Jesus the way to the Father*
Matthew 25.1–13   *The parable of the ten girls*
1 Corinthians 15.12–22   *Our resurrection*
Deuteronomy 30.15–20   *"Choose life"*
Psalm 34.11–22   *"Would you like to enjoy life?"*

24. Don't knock rock

I can't believe so many adults get worked up about rock music. I'll bet 99 per cent of the kids never even listen to the words. I don't. I might even know the words of some songs by heart, but I still don't really think about them that much. I'll admit some types of heavy metal are a bit over the top and some bands are definitely into Satan and all that but I still don't think anyone listens to their lyrics either.

Dave, 18

How do you feel about Dave's statement?

Strongly agree	Agree	Neutral	Disagree	Strongly disagree

- If you agree, what would you add to the statement above?
- If you disagree, why?

Suggested scripture to read

Matthew 13.1–23   *The parable of the sower*
2 Corinthians 6.14–18   *"How can right and wrong be partners?"*

25. Sex is for everyone

Nobody waits until they're married to have sex anymore. Nobody.
Except maybe somebody who grew up on an island where there wasn't
anybody of the opposite sex – or maybe somebody who lies a lot. Of
course, you have to be careful, but having sex is just a normal part of
relationships nowadays.

Sarah, 17

How do you feel about Sarah's statement?

Strongly agree	Agree	Neutral	Disagree	Strongly disagree

- If you agree, what would you add to the statement above?
- If you disagree, why?

Suggested scripture to read

1 Corinthians 6.12–20   *"Your body is the temple of the Holy Spirit"*
Matthew 5.27–30   *Teaching about adultery*
1 Corinthians 7.1–16   *Questions about marriage*

26. Suspicious parents

My parents are paranoid. Every time I come home from a party they want to know if there was any drinking or drugs. Well, of course there was. You can't go to a party anymore without someone drinking or smoking dope, but that doesn't mean I do, or even want to. I don't drink and I don't take drugs. My parents should believe me. If my parents knew what half of my friends did, they wouldn't let me have anything to do with them. But I can't tell my parents what really goes on; they'd lock me up and only let me out of the house to go to school and back. I wish they could just understand that they can trust me, and that what my friends do doesn't affect what I do.

Neil, 15

■ How would you feel if you were in Neil's position?
■ Why do you think you would feel that way?

Suggested scripture to read

Colossians 2.6–12   *Fullness of life in Christ*
Matthew 10.26–30   *Who to fear*
Ephesians 5.1–20   *Living in the light*

27. You can keep your stupid job

I work part-time in a burger restaurant. They pay me peanuts, just like everybody else. The manager treats me like dirt. I get the worst jobs, and he's always going on at me for every little mistake. If I need an evening or a weekend off to do something with my family, he won't give it to me. It's not as if this is my life's work. I'm not planning a career in fast food. I'm just working to get some spending money. And they're getting really cheap labour. They know that. They shouldn't try to take advantage of me by acting as if they're doing me a favour. I'm doing them a favour.

I asked for this next weekend off to go sailing, and the manager said no – so I resigned. There are plenty of other fast food places always looking for help.

George, 16

■ How would you feel if you were in George's position?
■ Why do you think you would feel that way?

Suggested scripture to read

Exodus 1.8–22   *The Israelites are treated cruelly in Egypt*
Ecclesiastes 11.9–10   *Advice to young people*
Romans 12.9–16   *"Love must be completely sincere"*
Ephesians 6.5–9   *Slaves and masters*

28. School isn't everything

My parents are more concerned about how I do at school than anything else in my life. They want me to go to college and so they're always going on at me to work for my A Levels. Well, I don't want to. School is OK and I'll probably get decent grades, but I'm fed up with the pressure. I don't see why I have to go to college anyway. In fact, a few of my friends and I are talking about earning some money and travelling around the world for a year after A Levels. Our parents are totally against the idea. Why? I don't think what you learn in school is everything. Besides, most of the teachers couldn't care less about my education. I really don't think you need to worry about A Levels. All I want to do at the moment is enjoy life and see a bit of the world. I've got the rest of my life to worry about work.

Andrew, 17

- How would you feel if you were in Andrew's position?
- Why do you think you would feel that way?

Suggested scripture to read

Proverbs 4.1–13   *The benefits of wisdom*
1 Timothy 4.12–16   *"Do not let anyone look down on you because you are young"*
Ecclesiastes 12.12   *"Too much study will wear you out"*

29. Hypocrites

Teenagers are so hypocritical. You have a lesson or video on racism or hunger, and everyone sits around crying and saying how concerned they are. Then a couple of days later, you see the same people making fun of some kid, or talking about all the new clothes they "need" right now. My friends only care about themselves. They say they're not going to be like their parents, that they are going to care about the world, and hunger, and the environment – but as soon as they're out of school, they're back to thinking about themselves full-time. None of my friends gives it a thought if they inconvenience their parents or ask for more money. In fact, they get angry if their parents won't go out of their way to help them. We're a bunch of spoiled, selfish, self-centred little brats. We pretend to care about the world, but really we don't care about anything except money, clothes, our friends, our music, and having a good time.

Suzi, 18

How do you feel about Suzi's statement?

Strongly   Agree   Neutral   Disagree   Strongly
agree   disagree

- If you agree, what would you add to the statement above?
- If you disagree, why?

Suggested scripture to read

Matthew 25.31–46   *The final judgement*
Matthew 19.16–26   *The rich young man*
1 John 3.13–18   *Love one another*

For further study or reflection

Ezekiel 33.30–33   *"They listen to all your words and don't obey a single one of them"*
James 2.14–18   *Faith and actions*

30. Old-fashioned

I guess I'm old-fashioned, but I really do think there's a hell. I believe that my friends need to accept Jesus. I don't want them to go to hell. I don't think I'm better than they are, and I don't think they're horrible people – I just care about them. I'm one of those weirdos that loves God. I care about my friends. I worry about them. I know that people who don't believe in Christ may be nice people, but they are never going to be really happy without him. Even though people make fun of me, I think I should try to tell all my friends about Jesus. And if they don't like it, that's all right – they still need to hear about him.

Bruce, 15

How do you feel about Bruce's statement?

Strongly   Agree   Neutral   Disagree   Strongly
agree   disagree

- If you agree, what would you add to the statement above?
- If you disagree, why?

Suggested scripture to read

Luke 16.19–31   *The rich man and Lazarus*
Ezekiel 33.1–9   *God appoints Ezekiel as a watchman*
Matthew 28.16–20   *The Great Commission*
2 Peter 3.8–15   *The promise of the Lord's coming*

31. The beautiful people

I go to a really exciting church. It is *the* place to go. We have about five hundred members and about seventy teenagers in the youth group. Everyone in the group is really popular at school. Our youth leader is Mr Stud – good looking, athletic, good speaker. We have a superb programme and fantastic weekends away. The adults in the church really support us, and we are respected in our town for our community service projects.

There's just one problem. The whole thing is a fraud. Maybe joke is a better word. Church has become just another social club for us. Everyone in the youth group hangs around together at school and goes to the same parties. There's not one bit of difference between the kids in our youth group and the rest of the people in school. They make fun of people, they swear, they drink, they watch violent videos. They do everything that everyone else does, except that they also go to church. At church they say all the right things. It's not as if they're being hypocrites; it's just that they don't see any problem – you go to church and behave one way, and you go to school and behave another way. I think it's a load of rubbish. Why go to church, if it's just another place to go? I don't go anymore. At least I feel more honest.

Joe, 16

How do you feel about Joe's statement?

Strongly   Agree   Neutral   Disagree   Strongly
agree   disagree

- If you agree, what would you add to the statement above?
- If you disagree, why?

Suggested scripture to read

Luke 9.1–6   *Jesus sends out the twelve disciples*
Hosea 6.1–7   *"I want your constant love"*
Isaiah 58.1–11   *True fasting*
Amos 5.21–24   *"I hate your religious festivals"*
Luke 18.9–14   *The Pharisee and the tax collector*

32. Porn ban

I have a friend who goes to a really strict church. Recently his youth group decided to protest at the sale of magazines like Playboy and Penthouse at the local newsagent. So they got together a big petition, and it worked – the shop decided to stop selling those magazines. I think it was stupid. I'm against pornography, but what's wrong with Playboy and Penthouse? We see just as much nudity in some of the videos we watch. And anyway, I don't think we should force what we believe on other people.

Nick, 16

How do you feel about Nick's statement?

Strongly   Agree   Neutral   Disagree   Strongly
agree   disagree

- If you agree, what would you add to the statement above?
- If you disagree, why?

Suggested scripture to read

Romans 1.18–32   *The guilt of mankind*
Matthew 5.27–30   *Teaching about adultery*
Luke 17.1–3   *Sin*

33. Just waiting

Yes, I like the fact that my parents have money. I like having a car, a nice house, and nice clothes. I enjoy all of those things. But if my parents think I'm going to be like them, they're wrong. I've made up my mind that, when I get older, I'm not going to join the rat race. I'm not going to get a job just so I can buy a house in suburbia, get my Volvo Estate, and have 2.3 kids. As soon as I leave college, I want to work in Africa with VSO or a similar organization, live simply, and give my life to helping people. I enjoy the good things in life, but I also hate what they do to me and my parents. I'm not going to let that happen. My parents would die if they knew how I really felt, so I don't tell them. I'm just waiting until I'm old enough to do what I want.

Ken, 16

■ How would you feel if you were in Ken's position?
■ Why do you think you would feel that way?

Suggested scripture to read

Luke 19.11–27   *The parable of the gold coins*
Luke 12.22–32   *Trust in God*
Luke 12.32–34   *Riches in heaven*
Luke 9.57–62   *The would-be followers of Jesus*
Luke 12.13–21   *The parable of the rich fool*

For further study or reflection

1 John 2.15–17   *"Do not love the world or anything that belongs to the world"*
1 Timothy 6.17–19   *"Command those who are rich not to be proud"*

part three:
tensions

The stories in this section require your youth group to think about the way each character in a story behaves.

34. Like father, like daughter

Carole's father was an alcoholic. At the moment, Mr Hancock was in work – although he had lost many jobs over the last few years. Mr Hancock was an after-work drinker. He would stop at his local on the way home from work and then come home and drink until he passed out in front of the television.

Carole never knew what to expect from him. Sometimes he would be angry and would verbally abuse anyone who was in the same room with him. Other times, he'd be very depressed. Then he would tearfully apologize to Carole and promise never to drink again. He would promise to take her shopping the next day and buy her lots of new clothes. But the promises were never kept.

Carole didn't know what to think of her mother. Most of the time she was very understanding. She would make excuses for her father and tuck him in at night. She never mentioned his drinking problems to others. But it was strange: every time Carole's father stopped drinking, her mother would become bitter. She would constantly shout at him, belittling him and calling him a failure and a slob, telling him about all the embarrassment and pain he had caused Carole and her. She would complain about the lack of money and accuse him of drinking their happiness away. So Carole's father would start drinking again, and Mrs Hancock would again become the perfect example of a loving and devoted wife.

Carole hated her father's drinking, and it was true that his drinking had cost the family a lot – but she also hated the way her mother acted when her father tried to stop drinking. Carole wondered, sometimes, whether her mother wanted her father to drink. She felt terrible for thinking such a thing, but she couldn't rid herself of those thoughts. Carole and her mother never talked about her father and his drinking. Once Carole suggested that they all go for counselling. Her mother flew into a rage and told Carole that it was her father who was sick, not them. They didn't need any help. Carole never brought it up again.

Carole tried to find help anyway. She went to her school teacher, who told her that alcoholism was a disease and that what her father needed was understanding, love, and medical help. Fine, Carole thought, but if it's just a disease, then why doesn't my father get medical help? Carole went to her youth leader at church. He said alcoholism was not a disease, it was a sin. He said the best thing Carole could do would be to pray for her father and get him to come to church. She tried. He wouldn't come.

Carole cared a lot for her father, but she had her own life to lead too. Carole felt pretty lucky to have a boyfriend like Rick. He was always there when she needed him, and lately she had needed him a lot. They were involved sexually, and that was because of Carole, not Rick. She needed the sexual closeness. When she and Rick had sex, she felt like all her problems were gone and nothing mattered except her and Rick. Rick was everything. She knew she loved him and that eventually they would get married. That's why she wasn't prepared when Rick said it was over. He said it was just that he didn't want to get tied down – that he didn't want to be so serious for a while. But Carole didn't believe him. She begged him to tell her what was really wrong. Finally, in frustration, Rick said that he was sick of her, that she smothered him. He was also tired of listening to her going on and on about her family problems. But the most painful thing he said was: "I hate sex with you. It's like you're using me. It's like sex is a drug, or something to help you escape from your problems. Well I'm tired of being used, and I'm tired of you."

Carole was devastated. She didn't know people could hurt so much. She walked out of school and ran home. No one was there. She was almost hysterical, and that frightened her. She didn't know what to do. And then she considered doing something she thought she would never do – resort to drinking. It would calm her down. She didn't even like the stuff, and one time surely couldn't hurt her. She found the wine in the fridge and poured herself a glass. It went down easier than she thought. She did feel better. She had one more and then another. Mrs Hancock came home at four in the afternoon. Carole was asleep on the couch (she'd passed out) with an almost empty bottle of wine on the floor.

- What went wrong?
- Think of the way each of the characters in the story behaved.
    Give them a "score" from   1 – OK
                                    to 10 – couldn't get much worse
- What grounds do you have for your opinion?

Suggested scripture to read

Ephesians 3.14–19   *The love of Christ*
1 Corinthians 6.12–20   *"Your body is the temple of the Holy Spirit"*
Galatians 6.1–10   *"Help to carry one another's burdens"*

35. Lovers lane

Teresa and Bill had been going out together for three years, and both of them were still virgins. That nearly ended one night recently. Luckily, they'd been interrupted by another couple driving to the same quiet spot.

Teresa was so upset she couldn't sleep. She really liked Bill a lot, and when she was older she wouldn't mind marrying someone like Bill. He was thoughtful, kind, intelligent (he could actually talk about something other than football and parties), and he wasn't pushy. Teresa believed that sex before marriage was wrong, but she also believed that getting pregnant was worse. She didn't believe in abortion, but the thought of having a baby while she was still at school was more than she could handle.

Teresa decided to be honest with her parents and talk about what she should do. She had always been very open with her parents; they'd been able to talk about everything. Teresa talked to her mum first: "Mum, I'm getting worried. Bill and I have been getting carried away. Don't panic, we haven't done anything yet, but I'm worried in case we do. Mum, what do you think about girls going on the pill?"

Mrs Reynolds replied, "Teresa, you know how much Dad and I like Bill and we're glad that you're going out together. The fact that you've told me about this tells me that you know that it's wrong, and I trust you both to do what you know is right. Besides, if both of you pray before you go out together, I believe God will help you. I don't believe in contraception before marriage, Teresa, and I really wouldn't like to think of you going on the pill."

Teresa's Dad surprised her. He suggested that she and Bill break up for a while to let things cool off. He said that, if they really loved each other, they could wait until they were both older. Teresa didn't like that answer at all.

At youth group that week, the discussion was about birth control. Steve, the youth leader, said that using contraception was like planning to sin. It was deciding that you probably would have sex. Steve said it was just a myth that all couples had sex, and that lots of people waited until marriage to have sex. Birth control was like saying that sex was inevitable, and planning on having sex before marriage was condoning it.

Bill and Teresa had a long talk that evening after youth group. They decided that sex before marriage was definitely wrong, and that they would take extra precautions to make sure they didn't get into a situation where they may go too far. But, secretly, Teresa had already made up her mind. She was going to have some kind of contraception. She decided to go to a family planning clinic where she could get any kind of contraception she wanted. She decided on the pill.

Two months later, the impossible happened. One afternoon after school, Bill and Teresa called in at her house to change for a swimming party, and before long they were in Teresa's bedroom having sex. Her parents were at work.

Bill panicked. Tearful and apologetic, he told Teresa that if she got pregnant she would have to get an abortion. Teresa couldn't believe it. Bill was against abortion – he hated abortion. Trying to calm him down, Teresa explained that there was no fear of her getting pregnant because she was on the pill.

That made Bill even more upset. He accused Teresa of planning the whole afternoon. He couldn't believe she was on the pill when they both agreed not to use it. Teresa responded, "Well, it's a good thing I was on the pill, or I might have had to face pregnancy alone, because you would have wanted me to get an abortion!"

"Teresa, if you lied about this, how do I know you haven't been lying about other things? Maybe you've been on the pill a lot longer than I know. Maybe I'm not the only one . . ." Bill didn't finish his sentence. He knew he'd gone too far.

Through her tears, Teresa told Bill to get out and never come back. He tried to apologize, but it was too late. He left. They didn't officially break up. They just never saw each other again.

- What do you think of the way each of the following people in the story behaved: Teresa, Bill, Mrs Reynolds, Mr Reynolds, youth leader?
- Give them a "score" from   1 – OK
                          to 10 – couldn't get much worse
- What grounds do you have for your opinion?

Suggested scripture to read

Romans 13.8–10   *"The only obligation you have is to love one another"*
1 John 4.15–18   *God is love*
James 1.12–18   *Testing and tempting*

36. One mistake

Paul had definitely made a stupid mistake. He had gone out with his friends and got drunk. He knew he shouldn't have, but sometimes things just got to him and he wanted to escape. Drinking was his way of escaping from his parents' divorce. At least that's what he always told himself. There had been other times, of course, but this was the first time he'd been caught.

His father banned him from using the car for a month as punishment. That was OK. He could take that. He deserved it.

But there was another problem: Ever since the night he'd got caught, his father and stepmother had changed. They didn't trust him any more. He'd expected that for a while, but it was going on too long. They never said they didn't trust him, of course; they would just check up on him all the time. They didn't believe him when he was late or when he explained why he had changed his plans. They continued to believe the worst anyway. It was an inconvenience, but not much more than that – until last Tuesday night.

Paul invited his best friend, Eric, to come over for the evening to his real mother's house. She was going to be away for a couple of days. They told Paul's father they were going to the cinema and then they were going to hire a video and watch it at his mother's house. His father asked whether they were going to invite anyone else, Paul said no.

Later, on his way up to the late-night shop, Paul's father drove by his ex-wife's house. Eric's car was there – which meant that Eric and Paul had not gone to the cinema. On his way back, he noticed that Eric's car was now gone, He drove into town and saw Eric's car outside the video shop. He parked his car and waited for them to leave. They left the shop, crossed the street to an off-licence, came out with a full carrier bag, got back in the car and returned to Paul's mother's house.

Paul's father also drove home. By now he was very suspicious. The boys had said they were going to rent a video – they had also said they were going to the cinema, which they had not. And what had they bought at the off-licence? As the evening wore on, he grew more and more uneasy. Finally, convinced that something was up, he decided to drive over to his ex-wife's house just to see if anything looked suspicious.

He parked his car and turned out the lights, just as a car pulled up to the house. Five girls got out of the car and walked up to the house, knocked, and went inside. Paul's father couldn't believe what he was seeing. A minute or two later, all the girls came out of the house, got back into the car and drove off.

Angry now, Paul's dad barged inside where he found Paul and Eric watching a video. "OK lads, I've got you this time. You didn't go to the cinema like you said."

"Yes, we did!"

"No, you didn't! Your car was right here. I saw it."

"I know, Dad, that's because we walked to the cinema."

"But when I drove past later, your car was gone!"

"That's because Eric left his wallet in the car."

"Yes, but you did go to the off-licence and you did have some girls in. You lied to me and I don't like it."

Paul stood up. "That's not true, Dad. The girls called in because they saw Eric's car in front of the house and they wanted us to go out for a drive with them. I told them we weren't allowed to have any girls over or go anywhere with them, so they left. Ask Eric." Paul knew that his dad would believe Eric. Embarrassed, Paul's dad apologized and left the two boys.

Relieved, Eric said that he'd really thought they were in trouble and that he couldn't believe Paul's father would actually admit he was wrong and apologize – after all, his father had never done that.

But Paul was furious. He didn't care whether his father had apologized or not. He said he was sick of his father holding one mistake over his head for the rest of his life. He was angry at his dad for making a scene in front of his friend. "Fine," he said, "If my dad thinks he can't trust me, then I might as well give him something to not trust me about. Let's invite some girls over, Eric – we'll have a party right now. And ask them to bring some drink." Eric went along with it. Actually, he'd always wanted the chance to have a wild party. Now, here it was – and he could always blame Paul if he was caught.

- What do you think of the way each of the following people in the story behaved: Paul, Eric, Paul's dad?
- Give them a "score" from   1 – OK
                                         to 10 – couldn't get much worse
- What grounds do you have for your opinion?

Suggested scripture to read

Colossians 3.12–17   *The old life and the new*
James 2.8–13   *Obey the law of the Kingdom*
Mark 10.42–50   *Temptations to sin*

37. The search

Mike's mother was searching his room when she heard Mike at the front door. She had found what she suspected to be some kind of illicit drug – a small packet of fine powder. She had decided to search his room when she'd overheard him talking to a friend on the phone about being "stoned". She was shocked. She had never dreamed this would happen to her son. This only happened to other people's kids.

She ran out to meet Mike in the hallway, holding the small package. Mike panicked. How did his mother find that? This wasn't supposed to happen. She was ruining everything. Why couldn't she leave him alone and let him make his own decisions? He didn't interfere with her life. He didn't say anything to her about the wine she drank at dinner or the bottles of spirit she kept in the cabinet. What gives her the right to tell him how to live? After all, Mike was seventeen years old.

Hysterically, she asked Mike what the "stuff" as she called it, was doing in his drawer. She flushed it down the toilet. Mike said nothing. His mother began crying uncontrollably. Mike walked into his room. It was a mess. His mother had gone through everything.

When she stopped crying, she walked into Mike's room and sat down next to him on the bed. She explained to him that she had searched his room because she loved him very much. She wanted to know the truth from him – what was that stuff?. It was very important to her and to their relationship. She tried to tell Mike that she understood how difficult things had been since the divorce. His father, who had moved away for business reasons, had not visited him for over three years. She wanted to know how she could make it up to him.

Mike decided to tell his mother the truth. He and a friend had been smoking cannabis at weekends for the past three months. His dope smoking was under control. He told his mother she had nothing to worry about. He smoked cannabis like she drank wine and spirits. He wouldn't become drug dependent, just as she wouldn't become an alcoholic.

His mum hit the roof. Screaming, she told Mike that he'd have to see a doctor or move out of the house.

And Mike had thought that telling the truth would get him off the hook. So much for telling the truth.

The doctor felt that Mike did have a drug problem, and that he was probably taking harder drugs than he admitted to. He recommended that Mike be placed in a drug rehabilitation centre.

After listening to the advice of the doctor, Mike's mother told Mike that he had the choice of getting treatment or moving out of the house.

Mike's father, when Mike called him to explain, said that it might be best for Mike if he came to live with him. Mike decided to move in with his dad.

- What do you think of the way each of the following people in the story behaved: Mike, Mike's father, Mike's mother, the doctor?
- Give them a "score" from   1 – OK
  to 10 – couldn't get much worse
- What grounds do you have for your opinion?

Suggested scripture to read

2 Corinthians 2.5–11   *Forgiveness for the offender*
Matthew 7.1–6   *"Do not judge others so that God will not judge you"*
Mark 2.13–17   *"I have not come to call respectable people but outcasts"*

38. Less than perfect

Phil rushed his wife, Diane, to the hospital. Her contractions were coming closer and closer together. The day they'd been so patiently awaiting had finally arrived – the birth of their first child. Despite his nervousness and excitement, Phil couldn't think of a happier moment in his life. Both he and Diane desperately wanted a child.

But afterwards, the obstetrics nurse had some painful news. The newborn baby girl had a genetic defect that was not correctable. The infant had visible deformities and moderate-to-severe brain damage. Phil and Diane were devastated. Diane wanted to hold her baby. Phil said no.

Then the doctor hurried into the room, a pained look on his face. "This is never an easy thing to discuss," he said in a low voice. He gave them a progress report: The baby might live, but it most definitely would not live a normal life. As they talked, the doctor wondered whether he should tell Diane and Phil any more. On the other hand, maybe he should do everything within his power to keep the child alive. But he finally suggested to Diane and Phil that they allow the infant to die. If they agreed, the hospital's normal procedure was to discontinue medical care and feeding of the infant.

At first Diane disagreed, but Phil insisted that they follow the doctor's advice. Reluctantly, she went along with Phil's decision. The doctor placed the order on the baby's medical chart. The obstetrics nurse, when she saw the doctor's orders, strongly disagreed – she felt the doctor was murdering an innocent, helpless child. She was quietly taken off the case. The baby died two days later.

- What do you think of the way each of the following people in the story behaved: Phil, Diane, the doctor, the baby, the obstetrics nurse?
- Give them a "score" from   1 – OK

   to 10 – couldn't get much worse
- What grounds do you have for your opinion?

Suggested scripture to read

John 9.1–5   *Jesus heals a blind man*
Matthew 18.1–5   *Who is the greatest?*
Psalm 139   *God's complete knowledge and care*

39. Parties

"Of course there'll be booze, Pam. It's going to be a party." Jeff handed Pam the map and walked to class.

Pam closed her locker and headed for class. Why do parties always have to include drinking? she wondered. She'd probably go since everyone she knew would be there. "It'll be all right, since I don't drink. Besides, the last party was fun. Hilary was there, and she acted so funny when she was drunk."

Pam's parents didn't like her going to parties where there was alcohol. But they didn't need to know about the booze. She wouldn't lie to them, but she wouldn't volunteer any information either.

When Pam got home that afternoon, she found a postcard from her church reminding her of the coming youth group social – the same night as Jeff's party. Her parents would encourage – no, would pressure her into attending the church social, which Pam knew would be boring. She wished her parents would get off her back about church things.

The day of the party, Pam's parents asked her what time she'd be home from the church social. She told them she wasn't in the mood for church activities and would prefer to go out with her girlfriends. Her parents reluctantly agreed. Pam went to the party with her girlfriends. Maybe she could keep them from getting too drunk.

- What do you think of the way each of the following people in the story behaved: Jeff, Pam, Hilary, Pam's parents, Pam's girlfriends?
- Give them a "score" from   1 – OK
                                        to 10 – couldn't get much worse
- What grounds do you have for your opinion?

Suggested scripture to read

Romans 16.17–20   *"Keep away..."*
Luke 11.33–36   *The light of the body*
1 Peter 3.13–17   *"Keep your conscience clear"*

40. Video nasty

Alan couldn't believe his eyes. Right there in the middle of the living room, his living room, was a video nasty on the TV. "Hey, Alan," said Mike, his older brother, "me and the lads are putting the video to good use while Mum's at work." Several of Mike's friends were scattered around the room. Mike smirked. "Oh, come on, Alan, don't look at me like that. Jack's joining the Navy, and we thought this would be a good send-off party for him." Jack, sprawled across the couch, was grinning. "It's only a film," Mike continued. "What's the problem? Mum'll never find out if you don't tell her. So why don't you get lost for the afternoon – and don't give me any of that Christian stuff."

As Alan left the house he could hear Mike and his friends laughing. He was ready to give up on his brother. He was a hopeless case. Mike used to go to church and youth group meetings. He'd even been president of the Christian Union at school once. But something had happened to Mike, and Alan didn't know what it could have been. It hadn't been his parents. They had done everything they could for Mike.

The next day, Mike apologized to Alan and asked him again not to tell their mother. He promised it wouldn't happen again. Sure, Alan thought, I've heard that before. He walked out of the room.

- What do you think of the way each of the following people in the story behaved: Alan, Mike, Mike's friends, Jack?
- Give them a "score" from 1 – OK
                            to 10 – couldn't get much worse
- What grounds do you have for your opinion?

Suggested scripture to read

Luke 6.37–42   *Judging others*
Philippians 4.4–9   *"Show a gentle attitude towards everyone"*
Matthew 18.15–17   *"If your brother sins against you . . ."*

41. The diary

Michelle's mother found the diary accidentally while she was cleaning Michelle's bedroom. She knew she shouldn't read it, but her curiosity got the better of her, and the next thing she knew she was reading her daughter's diary.

She was stunned. She could not believe that her daughter had written such things. She didn't think her daughter was capable of such anger toward her parents. Mrs Carson had always thought she and her daughter had a good relationship, but the things her daughter had said about her after some of their arguments shocked her. There was so much – too much to take at one time. She had no idea her daughter had ever had anything to drink, let alone got drunk. And the things she said about her boyfriends. Did young people really do things like that nowadays? Her own daughter? It was horrible. And the language. Mrs Carson had no idea her daughter ever used any swear words, let alone the ones she so freely used in her diary. Where had she learned such things?

Mrs Carson showed Michelle's diary to her husband. He was furious all right – but not with Michelle. He was furious with his wife for reading the diary. Still, he was shocked at what was in it. He didn't read it, but Mrs Carson had told him enough. Even though he believed Michelle's privacy had been violated, he also believed that something needed to be done about Michelle. How could they, as respectable parents, ignore what they knew?

The Carsons went to see their minister. They didn't bring the diary, but they did tell him they knew what was in it. The minister agreed with Mrs Carson's decision to read the diary. He believed that whatever parents have to do to help their child grow up is OK. If that means going through their drawers, their clothes, or their diaries to make sure they are telling the truth and not in trouble, then that's OK. "Parents have the right," the minister said, "to do whatever it takes to protect their children from the rough world out there."

The Carsons went home and confronted their daughter. Michelle completely fell apart. She couldn't believe that her own parents would violate her privacy and read her diary. The argument became so heated and ugly that Michelle left and went to stay with a friend. Her parents had no idea where she'd gone, but neither of them felt the least regret for what they had done; the fact the Michelle ran away only confirmed that they had done the right thing. Michelle knew she was wrong, they reasoned, and that is why she ran away. She'd be back.

- What do you think of the way each of the following people in the story behaved: Michelle, Mrs Carson, Mr Carson, Minister?
- Give them a "score" from   1 – OK
                          to 10 – couldn't get much worse
- What grounds do you have for your opinion?

Suggested scripture to read

Luke 15.11–32   *The lost son*
Matthew 10.26–27   *Who to fear*
Proverbs 22.6   *"Teach a child how he should live, and he will remember it all his life"*
Galatians 6.1–5   *Bear one another's burdens*
2 Corinthians 2.5–11   *Forgiveness for the offender*
Colossians 3.20–21   *Children and parents*

42. Secret birth control

Rachel didn't sleep around. She did sleep with her boyfriend, but that wasn't "sleeping around". It wasn't promiscuous – she really loved her boyfriend. She hoped someday they would get married. Ian wasn't the only boyfriend she had slept with, but people who love each other should have sex together. Sex is part of love.

Rachel was eighteen – old enough to make her own decisions. She had always tried to be honest with her parents. That doesn't mean she told them everything; there was such a thing as timing. Now that she was eighteen, she decided it was the right time to have a frank discussion with her parents (well, her mum anyway). She told her mum that she thought it was OK to have sex with someone you love and that, in fact, she had been having sex with Ian. She also told her mother that she thought abortion was wrong and therefore wanted to have birth control. Her mother was appalled at the whole conversation and refused to even discuss the possibility of birth control. She ordered Rachel to break up with Ian and not to have sex with anyone. Rachel reminded her mother that she could order birth control pills without her permission. Her mother threatened to destroy any birth control pills or devices she found.

Rachel continued having sex with Ian and acquired birth control pills through a local clinic. A couple of months later her mother found the pills and threw them away. Rachel was so angry that she continued to have sex with Ian without any protection. Two months later she discovered she was pregnant. Since she didn't believe in abortion, she told Ian she was pregnant, fully expecting him to agree to get married. After all, they had been talking about it. She was shocked to discover he had no intention of getting married and blamed her for getting pregnant in the first place.

"If you had used birth control pills, we wouldn't be in this mess," he told her.

"Well, what about you!" she yelled. "Why didn't you use protection?"

Ian replied sarcastically, "Because I'm not the one who can get pregnant!"

Rachel broke up with Ian and had a secret abortion. All her parents knew was that she had broken up with Ian. They were very proud of Rachel and glad to see that she had responded to their wishes.

- What do you think of the way each of the following people in the story behaved: Rachel, Ian, Rachel's mum?
- Give them a "score" from   1 – OK
                             to 10 – couldn't get much worse

■ What grounds do you have for your opinion?

Suggested scripture to read

1 Corinthians 13.1–13   *Love*
Ephesians 6.1–4   *Parents and children*
Luke 11.37–41   *Jesus and the Pharisees*
Galatians 6.7–10   *"A person will reap exactly what he sows"*

43. The quitter

Bob received a car for his eighteenth birthday. His parents told him he'd have to pay for the petrol and insurance for the car himself – he'd been doing a part-time job in a garage for almost a year. If it weren't for that, they wouldn't have been able to afford the car.

What they didn't know was that Bob hated his job. He was earning the minimum wage, and his boss was treating him like dirt making him do all the jobs that the others didn't want to do. He was always at the bottom of the pile when it came to drawing up the rota, as well. They would often tell him he had to work Friday and Saturday nights, and then when he arrived, tell him they needed him for only an hour or they didn't need him at all. When work was extra busy, they'd make him stay late and lock up because the others "had plans". Bob had been planning to leave for a long time. Of course, he was excited about the car – but he also wanted to finish with the job.

After he'd had the car a month, he told his parents he wanted to leave work. His parents were very upset. Bob explained that he was being mistreated at work and that his boss refused to listen to his complaints. But his parents insisted that they bought the car with the expectation that Bob would pay for its upkeep. "It's too late," Bob shrugged. "I've already given my notice." His father angrily called Bob's boss, who told him that if Bob hadn't given his notice, he would have been fired for his terrible attitude and his laziness.

Furious now, Bob's dad accused Bob of being irresponsible, lazy, and selfish – and dishonest, because he misled his parents until after they bought the car. "If you leave your job," he said, "I'll sell the car."

Bob, devastated, insisted that his boss wasn't telling the truth. "I'm not lazy," he told his father. "I just don't like being treated like a slave. And remember – I worked six months longer than I wanted to, just to prove that I'm not lazy or irresponsible."

His parents refused to accept his explanation. "The real world out there isn't very friendly," they explained. "Many people have to work at jobs they don't like. Sometimes adults have to do what they don't want to do just to survive."

"I understand all that," Bob said. "But sometimes you have to stand up to people who mistreat you. I don't want to ignore my responsibilities; I just want to be treated like a human being."

His parents gave him an ultimatum: Work or no car. Bob left his job. His parents sold the car.

■ What do you think of the way each of the following people in the story behaved: Bob, Bob's parents, Bob's boss?

- Give them a "score" from 1 – OK
                        to 10 – couldn't get much worse
- What grounds do you have for your opinion?

Suggested scripture to read

Matthew 20.1–16   *The workers in the vineyard*
Amos 5.10–15   *"You people hate anyone who challenges injustice and speaks the whole truth in court"*
Ecclesiastes 11.9–10   *Advice to young people*
Romans 12.9–16   *"Love must be completely sincere"*

44. Fatso

Sue was basically a happy girl – in the fifth year at school, good looking, slim. Everything was going great, and then the bottom fell out of her world. Not only were her parents divorced, but her mother remarried almost immediately. Everyone at school knew about the divorce and knew that Sue's mum was involved with another man before the divorce. Sue didn't get along well with her real father, but she hated Gary, her new stepfather. She understood why her mother wanted to get a divorce, but after she met Gary, her mother had no time for Sue – all she could think about was him. Sue felt that she was in the way, and when she asked her mother about it, her mother would simply say that Sue was over-reacting and not being very understanding.

Sue thought about going to live with her real father but decided against it for a number of reasons. First, she didn't get along with her father, although she did feel sorry for him because her mum had been unfaithful. And second, Sue's mother had made it very clear that if Sue went with her father, it would be considered a betrayal.

Sue was depressed. And she quickly discovered that eating helped. She didn't notice it at first, but gradually she realized she was eating all the time and gaining weight. Lots of weight. The more weight she gained, the more Sue's mum complained. There were times when her mother threatened to send Sue to her father's if she didn't stop. In fact, Sue called her father and asked whether she could live with him. He said no – he had his own life to live, and besides, if she was as heavy as everyone said then she had better quit worrying about where to live and start losing weight instead.

Sue just kept eating. One day her church youth leader stopped by and told Sue he was concerned about her. Sue felt like she could trust him, so she told him all about the family problems that had led to her overeating. He told Sue that all she needed to do was pray and ask God to take away the desire to eat. Sue did pray for about six months – she gained another five pounds.

At least she still had her boyfriend. She'd been going steady with Martin for almost two years. She was relieved that he still cared for her despite her weight problem. Then the worst happened – Sue found a note in Martin's car that he had written to a friend. It said:

Bob, I've got to work out how to finish with Sue, quick, without hurting her feelings. I just don't fancy her anymore.

The next day Sue swallowed a whole bottle of sleeping pills.

- What went wrong?
- Think of the way each of the characters in the story behaved.

- Give them a "score" from   1 – OK
                        to 10 – couldn't get much worse
- What grounds do you have for your opinion?

Suggested scripture to read

Matthew 20.1–16   *Workers in the vineyard*
Philippians 2.1–11   *"Your life in Christ makes you strong"*

___ part four: ___
dear diary

These fictional "diary entries" are intimate, no-holds-barred statements of adolescent feelings. Have your youth group read these "confidential" writings and then respond to them.

45. Heart-throb

Dear Diary,

Today was so great! Graham Armstrong wants to go out with me. He is gorgeous. And he's 18! I can't believe it. Any girl in school would give her virginity away for him – and he likes me. I am *so* happy. Heather is jealous and being a real bitch. I don't care. Of course, it's going to take some real doing to pull this off. You know why! My parents are so old-fashioned! They don't want me going out with older boys. My parents seem to think that all boys want is sex. Well, they're wrong. Graham is the nicest person I have ever met and I am not going to let him go. I mean, I wouldn't even mind going too far with him, he's so lovely. And besides, if I'm going to keep him around for four years, we can't exactly hold hands. Seriously, Diary, I would marry him right now. Of course I can't, I'm only fifteen – but my mum was eighteen when she married my dad. Whoops, I've got to go, that will be Graham at the door.

Tina

- What should Tina do?
- What should Tina's parents do?
- What would you do?

Suggested scripture to read

Luke 12.13–21   *The parable of the rich fool*
Matthew 13.44–46   *The parables of the hidden treasure and the pearl*
Galatians 5.16–26   *"Let the Spirit direct your lives"*

46. Totally ugly

Dear Diary,

It's me again. The ugliest girl in the school. Do you know how many boys have asked me out in four years? None! Everyone in the world gets asked out at least once, or has a boyfriend. I suppose you've got to be really ugly to never be asked out. My parents are so stupid. Now they're telling me how great I am. Just because my GCSE results are so good. They don't even care about my social life. They act as if that doesn't matter as long as I do well at school. I don't mind being clever, but I would much rather have a boyfriend and be completely stupid. Sometimes I wish I was dead.

What really gets me, is they keep saying it doesn't matter what you look like, it's what's inside that matters. Fine. The trouble is, no one in the entire universe believes that. Besides, that tells me what they think of me. They do think I'm ugly! There is nothing worse than being ugly. Nothing.

Janet

- What advice would you give Janet?
- What advice would you give Janet's parents?
- What would you do if you were Janet?

Suggested scripture to read

Isaiah 43.1–7   *"Do not be afraid – I will save you"*
Matthew 25.14–30   *The parable of the three servants*
1 Corinthians 12.4–26   *Gifts from the Holy Spirit*

47. No problem

Dear Diary,

I can't believe how worried everyone is about AIDS. They act as if we're all going to get it. First of all, you can't get AIDS unless you're homosexual, a drug addict, or you sleep around with a million different people. Our minister at church actually said tonight that the only way to protect yourself from AIDS is not to have sex with anyone until you're married. But how do you know that the person you are going to marry hasn't had sex with someone else? And that person with two or three other people. And each of those with others etc. I don't think it matters who you have sex with as long as you protect yourself with a condom. I suppose when I think about it though, I would prefer to marry a virgin. At least then you're sure you're safe.

Philip

- Do you agree or disagree with Philip? Explain your view.
- Do you agree or disagree with Philip's minister? Explain your view.

Suggested scripture to read

Philippians 3.18–21   *"Their god is their bodily desires"*
Ephesians 5.1–20   *Living in the light*
Galatians 6.7–10   *"A person will reap exactly what he sows"*

48. The wally

Dear Diary,

Why is my brother such a wally? He's always using my stuff, ruining my tapes, and losing half my clothes. My parents think he's about the most wonderful person in the world, and that I'm the troublemaker. If they only knew. He lies to them all the time, he uses their credit cards without their permission, he drinks like a fish – and my parents think he's Mr Innocent! I can't believe it. Sometimes I hate my brother, and other times I feel sorry for him. He's so selfish. He uses them. He uses me. So how come I don't let my parents know the truth about him? Because I'm not a sneak. And anyway, my parents wouldn't believe me. I'm going to be really glad when he gets out of the house. I wish he were leaving today.

Julian

- What advice would you give to Julian?
- What advice would you give to Julian's brother?
- If Julian's parents had read this diary entry, what would you advise them to do?

Suggested scripture to read

James 3.13–18   *"Where there is jealousy and selfishness there is also disorder"*

Genesis 37.1–7   *Joseph and his brothers*

Matthew 18.21–35   *The parable of the unforgiving servant*

49. The funeral

Dear Diary,

Gary Hill was involved in a terrible accident last night. He ran off the road and was killed. It was pretty horrible. I didn't know him all that well, but he was popular in school and loads of people were devastated today. It seemed every girl in the school was crying. His funeral is in a couple of days and the school is going to let everyone go. Yuck! Funerals! Horrible. Why would anyone want to go to a funeral? I mean, I didn't know him that well. I think everyone's going just to get out of school. Maybe they're going because it's the nice thing to do. But lots of people will go who didn't really care about Gary and they'll have forgotten him in a couple of weeks. Besides, I think funerals are for old people. If you're dead, you're dead. Why sit around and look at a coffin? I would rather have everyone remember me as I was. I'm never going to have a funeral.

Teresa

- Do you agree with Teresa's opinion of funerals?
- What advice would you give to Teresa?

Suggested scripture to read

Ecclesiastes 3.1–8 *A time for everything*
Luke 7.11–17 *Jesus raises a widow's son*
John 20.1–2; 11–18 *The empty tomb*
1 Thessalonians 4.13–14 *The Lord's coming*
Matthew 5.1–12 *"Happy are those who mourn"*

50. Teenage mum

Dear Diary,

I can't believe my mum. It's as if she thinks she's sixteen or something. I need so many new clothes and I come home today and she's dressed up like a teenager. She looks better than I do! I'm serious. When I say something like I think she looks ridiculous or I think she looks too young, she goes crazy. She gets all angry and says that everyone dresses like that – which they don't. She says that she has the right, after all these years, to buy herself some clothes, and that it's OK for a mum to want to look nice. She doesn't even listen. It's embarrassing. And she's always wanting me to invite all the "girls" over so we can do something together. Can you believe it? I don't want my mum to do things with me and the girls. I've even tried to talk to Dad about it. Do you know what he says? "I like your mum to look young." It's sick! Why don't they just try and look like a mum and dad instead of trying to looking like they're still in their teens?

Becky

- What should Becky do?
- What should Becky's mum do?
- What would you tell Becky's dad?

Suggested scripture to read

Colossians 3.12–17   *"Be tolerant with one another"*
Ephesians 6.1–4   *Children and parents*
Ecclesiastes 3.1–8   *A time for everything*
1 Peter 3.3–6   *"Your beauty should consist of your true inner self"*
Proverbs 30.17   *"Anyone who makes fun of his father . . ."*

index